This journal belongs to:

____

Made in the USA
Middletown, DE
30 January 2023

23602585R00068